Part of the wall between the field and the hill has fallen down.
Three sheep creep into the field.

They find a gap in the hedge at the bottom of the field. They creep onto the grass next to the road.

The sheep munch the long grass next to the road. A car comes down the road. 'Beep, beep. Beep, beep.'

The horn startles the sheep. They jump up. They stamp in a panic. 'Baa, baa, baa.'

One of the sheep lands in a ditch.

'Baa, baa.' The sheep cannot get out of the ditch. 'Baa, baa.'

Wellington and Kevin go to see what is the matter. Wellington sends Kevin to fetch the farmer.

Wellington looks after the sheep until the farmer comes. The farmer pulls the sheep out of the ditch.

Wellington and Kevin push the sheep back over the wall. Then the farmer mends the wall to keep his sheep on the hill.